# Crabapples

# Sea Otters

## Bobbie Kalman

Crabtree Publishing Company

# Crabapples

## created by Bobbie Kalman

### For Priscilla and Karl Baker

**Editor-in-Chief**
Bobbie Kalman

**Writing team**
Bobbie Kalman
Hannelore Sotzek

**Managing editor**
Lynda Hale

**Editors**
Niki Walker
Petrina Gentile
Greg Nickles

**Computer design**
Rose Campbell

**Color separations and film**
Dot 'n Line Image Inc.

**Special thanks to**
Ken Peterson, Michell Staedler, Nicole Amato and the Monterey Bay
Aquarium; Ellen Faurot-Daniels and Friends of the Sea Otter

**Illustrations**
Barbara Bedell: pages 6-7

**Photographs**
Jack Ames/Friends of the Sea Otter: page 29 (bottom)
Frank S. Balthis: pages 18, 19, 31
Robert E. Barber: pages 8-9, 23, 24-25
Tom Campbell: page 26
John Cancalosi/Tom Stack & Associates: pages 12, 16-17
Jeff Foott: cover, title page, pages 4-5 (both), 9 (bottom),
    10, 11, 13, 15, 20, 21, 27, 28-29, 30
Jeff Foott/Tom Stack & Associates: pages 14, 22
Norbert Wu: page 16

**Printer**
Worzalla Publishing Company

## Crabtree Publishing Company

| | | |
|---|---|---|
| 350 Fifth Avenue | 360 York Road, RR 4, | 73 Lime Walk |
| Suite 3308 | Niagara-on-the-Lake, | Headington |
| New York | Ontario, Canada | Oxford OX3 7AD |
| N.Y. 10118 | L0S 1J0 | United Kingdom |

**Cataloging in Publication Data**
Kalman, Bobbie
  Sea otters

(Crabapples)
Includes index.

ISBN 0-86505-634-X (library bound)  ISBN 0-86505-734-6 (pbk.)
This book examines the biology and habitats of sea otters,
as well as behaviors such as hunting, playing, and mating.

1. Sea otter - Juvenile literature. I. Title. II. Series: Kalman,
Bobbie. Crabapples.

QL737.C25K34 1996          j599.74'447          LC 96-36375
                                                          CIP

# What is in this book?

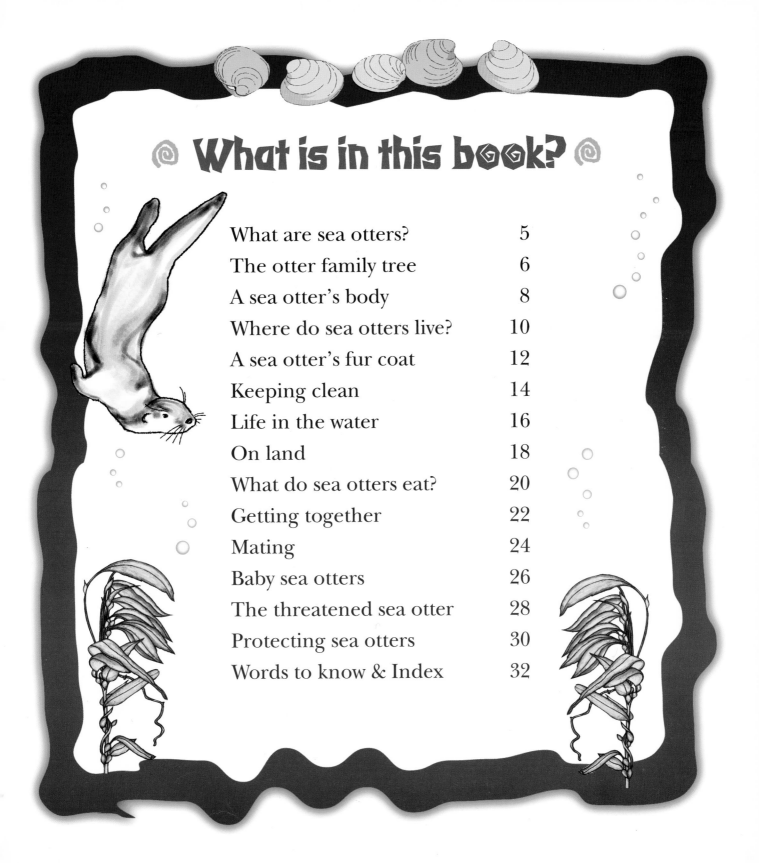

What are sea otters?               5

The otter family tree              6

A sea otter's body                 8

Where do sea otters live?          10

A sea otter's fur coat             12

Keeping clean                      14

Life in the water                  16

On land                            18

What do sea otters eat?            20

Getting together                   22

Mating                             24

Baby sea otters                    26

The threatened sea otter           28

Protecting sea otters              30

Words to know & Index              32

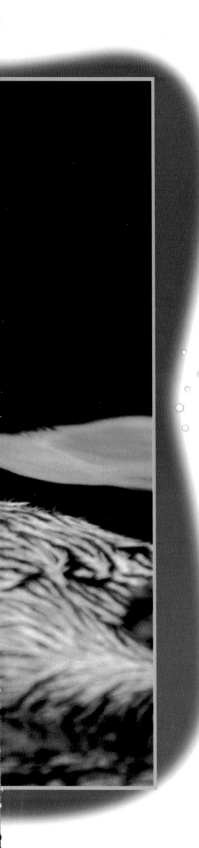

# What are sea otters?

Sea otters are **mammals**. They are **warm-blooded**. A mammal's body temperature stays the same in both warm and cold surroundings. Mammals have fur or hair. A baby mammal feeds on its mother's milk. Sea otters are **marine** mammals. They live only in salt water. Dolphins and whales are also marine mammals. Even though these mammals live in water, they have lungs and breathe above the water.

# The otter family tree

Otters are members of the **mustelid** family. Most otters live on land and spend some time in rivers and lakes. The North American river otter, the Asian clawless otter, and the Brazilian giant otter are examples of freshwater otters.

Two types of otters live only in water—the northern sea otter and the southern sea otter. Both live in salt water.

North American river otter

Asian clawless otter

northern sea otter

southern sea otter

Brazilian giant otter

Scientists believe that the sea otter's ancestor was a land mammal that lived millions of years ago. The animal had to fight for food along the shoreline but not in the ocean. The ancestor spent more and more time in the water until the ocean became its home.

weasel

badger

skunk

mink

Otters belong to the same family as weasels, badgers, skunks, and minks. Most mustelids have special scent glands near their tail. These glands release a liquid that is used for defense or marking territory.

# A sea otter's body

A sea otter's body is designed for living in the water. The otter has large lungs that hold lots of air. With one breath, a sea otter can stay underwater for almost five minutes! An otter's backbone, or **spine**, bends easily, allowing the animal to dive and somersault in the water. When a sea otter dives, its nostrils and ears clamp shut to keep out water.

Sea otters use their flippers for swimming. The long webbed toes on these large hind feet help an otter swim quickly.

A sea otter steers through the water with its thick, flat tail.

8

A sea otter's eyes and nose are high on its head, so the otter can see and breathe easily when it is floating.

Sea otters have a thin layer of film over their eyes. This film keeps salt water from stinging the eyes.

Whiskers help sea otters feel their surroundings. Sea otters also use their whiskers to search for food.

Sea otters rely on their front paws to find and eat food and to clean themselves. Sea otters do not use their front paws for swimming.

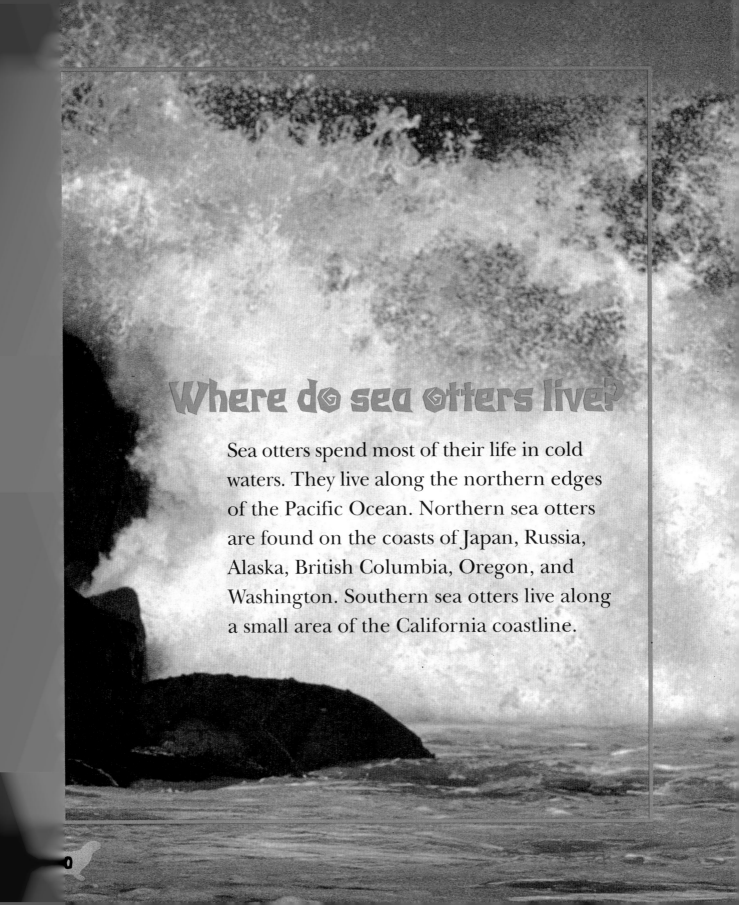

# Where do sea otters live?

Sea otters spend most of their life in cold waters. They live along the northern edges of the Pacific Ocean. Northern sea otters are found on the coasts of Japan, Russia, Alaska, British Columbia, Oregon, and Washington. Southern sea otters live along a small area of the California coastline.

Sea otters usually stay close to the shore, where the water is not too deep. In shallow waters, the otters can dive easily to the ocean floor to search for prey. Big rocks along the shoreline help protect sea otters from strong winds and waves.

RUSSIA

Alaska

CANADA

Pacific Ocean

JAPAN

UNITED STATES

# A sea otter's fur coat

Sea otters must keep their body warm even when the water around them is cold. Most marine mammals have a thick layer of fat, called **blubber**, under their skin to keep them warm. The sea otter does not have blubber. It relies on its fur for warmth in cold waters.

A sea otter's fur coat has two layers: **guard hairs** and **underfur**. The long guard hairs grow so closely together that only their tips get wet. They protect the short underfur from the water. Air trapped between the layers of fur helps keep the otter warm.

Only a few parts of an otter's body do not have fur—its nose, ears, lips, and the bottoms of its paws. When it floats, the otter keeps these parts above the cold water.

# Keeping clean

It is important for the sea otter to clean, or **groom**, its fur often. When the fur is dirty, the guard hairs clump together, and the underfur and skin get wet.

Body heat trapped between the layers of fur escapes, and the sea otter becomes cold. Being chilled can cause the sea otter to get sick or even die.

A sea otter cleans its fur several times a day. With its tongue and front paws, the otter frees any dirt in its fur. It pulls and stretches its loose skin to reach every part of its body. The otter then dives, rolls, and somersaults in the water to rinse itself.

After rinsing, the sea otter blows dry its thick coat with its nose and mouth! The otter then carefully combs and fluffs its fur using its teeth and front claws.

# Life in the water

Sea otters are expert swimmers. When it dives, a sea otter often stays underwater for as long as one to two minutes. On top of the water, a sea otter floats and swims on its back. It paddles with its hind feet to push itself through the water.

Many sea otters even sleep on the water! When floating, they usually wrap themselves in a type of seaweed called **kelp**. Kelp sometimes acts as a barrier. Most predators, such as orcas, cannot swim through the kelp beds. Sea otters also use kelp as an anchor. They twist their body in the seaweed to keep from drifting far out to sea while they are sleeping.

 ## ◎n land

Sea otters leave the water when they are cold or threatened by enemies. They climb onto land or rocks. Going ashore is called **hauling out**. Northern sea otters sometimes haul out to eat, sleep, and groom themselves. Southern sea otters rarely leave the water.

Sea otters move slowly and awkwardly on land. They often trip over their large hind feet. Land predators, such as brown bears, stalk the shoreline and search for the slow-moving sea otters. The otters stay close to the water so they can dive in quickly and swim to safety.

# What do sea otters eat?

Sea otters are **carnivores**—they eat meat. Sea otters can eat up to forty different types of seafood, including sea stars, sea urchins, clams, crabs, mussels, and snails. Most sea otters, however, prefer to eat only two to four types of meat. These favorite foods are usually the same ones their mother ate.

A sea otter floats on its back when it is eating. It uses its chest as a table. Sometimes an otter's prey has a shell that covers the soft meat. To break open the shell, the otter places a rock on its chest and hits the prey against it.

Sea otters are always eating! They must eat up to one-quarter of their body weight in food each day. How much would you have to eat if you were a sea otter?

# Getting together

Most sea otters enjoy swimming and playing together. They often gather in groups called **rafts**. When sea otters float together, they are **rafting**.

Male sea otters usually stay with other males, and females often raft with females. Some otters do not join a raft. They prefer to swim and float alone.

Sea otters communicate with one another by shrieking and squealing. They make these noises during play, when they are hungry, and when they want attention. Some sea otters also make noises to warn the rest of their raft when danger is nearby.

Baby sea otters shriek and squeal very loudly when they are separated from their mother. A mother can find her baby by following its cries.

# Mating

Sea otters must mate to have babies. Most adult male and female otters spend time together only to mate. Mating can happen at any time of the year. It may last for one day or for several days.

A male swims up to a female to see if she is willing to mate. If she is not, she lets him know by making hissing sounds and slapping him. If she wants to mate, the female otter allows the male to come closer.

When they begin to mate, the otters tumble, roll, and splash together in the water. Soon their play becomes rough, however. The male otter grabs the female and bites her on the nose. The female otter's wet fur is slippery, and biting her nose gives him a firm grip. His bite also gives the female a bloody nose!

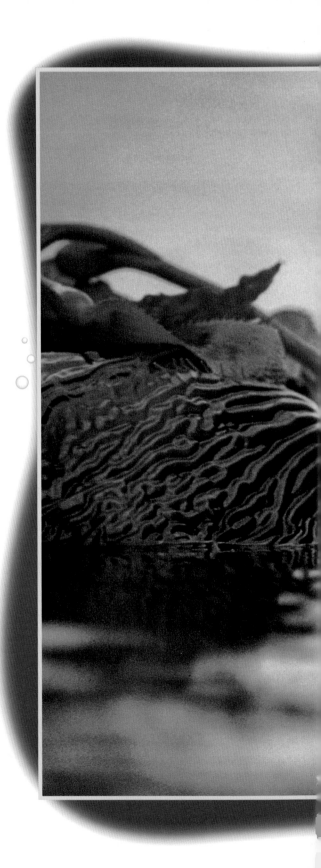

# Baby sea otters

Baby sea otters are called **pups**.
Northern sea otter pups are often
born on land, but southern ones are
usually born in the water.

Most mothers give birth to only one
pup. If twins are born, the mother cares
for one and leaves the other on its own.
She cannot care for two pups at once.

To guard the pup and keep it warm, the mother carries it on her chest. She grooms her pup several times a day. She feeds it milk from her body until the pup is a few weeks old. She then begins to share her prey with it. Most pups leave their mother when they are between the ages of five and eight months.

Sea otter pups like to dive, somersault, and chase one another. They are curious about their surroundings. Young otters examine everything within their reach.

# The threatened sea otter

In the past, people hunted sea otters for their thick fur. Eventually, laws were passed to stop the hunting of these animals. The number of sea otters has grown since then, but many of these animals are still in danger. Storms, people, pollution, and diseases threaten their survival. Fishers drag nets to catch fish, but they also catch sea mammals. Many sea otters drown when they are tangled in the fishing nets and cannot get to the surface to breathe air.

Oil spills are very dangerous to sea otters. The oil mats their fur, causing the otters to become wet and cold. The animals are poisoned by the oil when they lick their fur. They are also harmed by eating oil-covered shellfish.

Today, southern sea otters are a **threatened species**. To be classified as threatened means that people must protect these animals so they do not become **extinct**. When a species becomes extinct, it disappears from the earth forever.

# Protecting sea otters

Many people want to protect sea otters. Some groups rescue orphaned sea otter pups. People dive with the babies, training them to find food and crack open shellfish with a rock. When the pup is able to find food on its own, the trainers return the otter to the ocean.

Some groups also try to move sea otters away from areas where oil is often spilled. When otters, such as the one on page 29, are covered in oil, people rescue them and try to remove it from their fur. They hope that the otters can be cleaned before the oil makes them sick. Otters that do become ill are cared for until they are well. They are then released into the wild.

# Words to know

**ancestor** Something from which something or someone is descended

**barrier** Something that blocks the movement of something or someone

**blubber** A thick layer of fat under an animal's skin

**carnivore** An animal that eats only meat

**fresh water** Water that is not salty

**gland** A sac inside the body that produces a liquid

**hauling out** The action of leaving the water to go on land

**mammal** A warm-blooded animal that has a backbone

**marine** Describing something that comes from or lives in the sea

**orphan** A young child or creature whose parents are dead

**predator** An animal that hunts other animals for food

**prey** An animal hunted by another animal for food

**rafting** The action of otters floating together

# Index

ancestor 7
babies 5, 23, 24, 26-27, 30
body 8-9, 12, 13, 15, 17, 27
breathing 5, 8, 9, 28
communication 23, 24
danger 23, 28-29
defense 7, 17, 18, 23
diving 8, 11, 15, 16, 18, 27, 30
eating 9, 18, 20-21, 29
feet 8, 9, 13, 15, 16, 18
floating 9, 13, 16, 17, 21, 22
food 5, 7, 9, 20-21, 27, 29, 30

fur 5, 12-13, 14, 15, 24, 28, 29, 31
grooming 9, 14-15, 18, 27
habitat 5, 6, 10-11
keeping warm 12, 13, 27
mammals 5, 7, 12, 28
mating 24
mothers 5, 20, 23, 26, 27
northern sea otter 6, 10, 18, 26
nose 9, 13, 15, 24
oil spills 29, 31

on land 6, 18, 26
otter family tree 6-7
play 22, 23, 24, 27
predators 17, 18
prey 11, 21, 27
protection 11, 27, 29, 30-31
sickness 14, 28, 31
sleeping 17, 18
southern sea otter 6, 10, 18, 26, 29
swimming 8, 9, 16, 18, 22
using tools 21, 30